Behind the Scenes in a
DEPARTMENT STORE

Behind the Scenes in a

DEPARTMENT STORE

by LEON HARRIS

with photographs by the author

J. B. LIPPINCOTT COMPANY / Philadelphia   New York

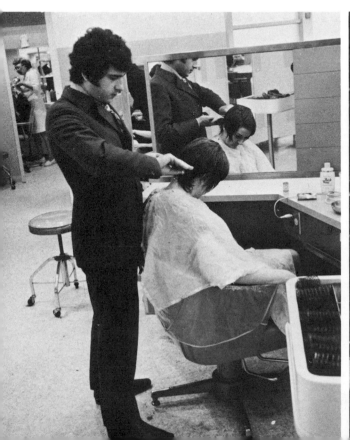

Acknowledgments

For their kind permission to use the photographs found on the pages listed after their names, the author wishes to thank Neiman Marcus—2 (left), 17 (top), 21 (right), 24, and back cover upper right; the National Housewares Manufacturers Association—17 (bottom); and Macy's—3 (right), 8, 12 (bottom), 19, 26, 27, 33, 34, 39, 42, and back cover lower right. All other photographs are by the author. He is especially grateful to Miss Sabom, Miss Moss, and Mr. Briggle of that *ne plus ultra* of stores, Neiman Marcus.

U.S. Library of Congress Cataloging in Publication Data

Harris, Leon A
   Behind the scenes in a department store.

   SUMMARY: Describes the services and duties of the staff in the various sales, maintenance, administrative, and other behind-the-scenes areas of a department store.

   1. Department stores—Juvenile literature. 2. Department stores—Employees—Juvenile literature. [1. Department stores] I. Title.
PZ9.H27Be   658.87′1   70-151487
ISBN-0-397-31221-0

Office of

Harris & Co.

A. HARRIS.
S. MARCUS.

DRY GOODS, DRAPERIES AND LADIES WEAR.

NEW YORK OFFICE,
9 LISPENARD ST.

266-268 & 270 ELM ST.
COR. MURPHY.

Dallas, Texas, Nov 12 1900

Folio 30

Sold to Mrs R Leibman

ALL BILLS ARE PAYABLE MONTHLY.

DATE.			CHARGES.	CREDITS.
Oct	1	To Balance A/c Rend	119 72	
		Diftm Suit 600 Supp 15 6 Pins 20 & D Coll 5		
		4 Embr 35 140 3 Hose 100 1 Dr 150 8 Embr 35 280	13 10	
	6	4 Vests 75	3 00	
	13	1 Suit	21 50	
	15	1 Rem Embr 75 120 70 12 Dr 60	2 05	
	16	1 Waist 550 1½ Rib 65 ½ Dr 30	6 45	
	17	1¼ Rib	40	
	20	1 Corset 500 1 Tie 85	5 85	
	23	4 Shades hung 100 400 2 Do 90 180 1 Do 50 1 Do 175 1 Waist 850	16 55	
	29	½ Embr 18 9 4 Vests 75 300 1 Shade 175 hung 2 Do 100 200 1 Do 90	7 74	
			196 36	
	18	By 1 Waist Returned		5 50
			190 86	
Nov	12	By def on Suit 600 int 32		6 32
		Bal.		184 54

This book is for
A. H.
and
L. A. H.
and
all A. Harris people
with gratitude.

Behind the Scenes in a
DEPARTMENT STORE

Most great department stores started out very small. A peddler with a pack on his back graduated to a pushcart and then to a horse and wagon and finally moved into a hole-in-the-wall shop which slowly grew. In the main, these shops grew because the owners tried to give fair value and quality for the money and because they put price tags on their merchandise and stuck to the stated price, at a time when other merchants bargained and argued with customers about the price of each item. In the one-price shops, the customers knew that whether or not they were getting a bargain, at least they were paying no more than anyone else.

Little by little these shops increased the kinds of merchandise they carried until they grew into full department stores. As cities in America became larger and more spread out, the big downtown stores built branch stores out in the suburbs where their customers lived. The department store has become a large enterprise which needs a wide variety of people of differing talents.

From the moment a customer walks into a store, everything is designed to induce him or her to buy—imaginative displays, demonstrations showing how products work, clear signs, and good lighting—and all this is possible because of many different hands and minds working together.

To the customer, the most important human in the store is his salesperson. If the salesperson is pleasant and knowledgeable, the customer likes the store. Salespeople need a lot of training before meeting the public. Not only should they know the basics of their work, how their stock is arranged, how to write a sales ticket, and how to use a cash register, but also very often they should have specialized knowledge about the kind of merchandise they sell.

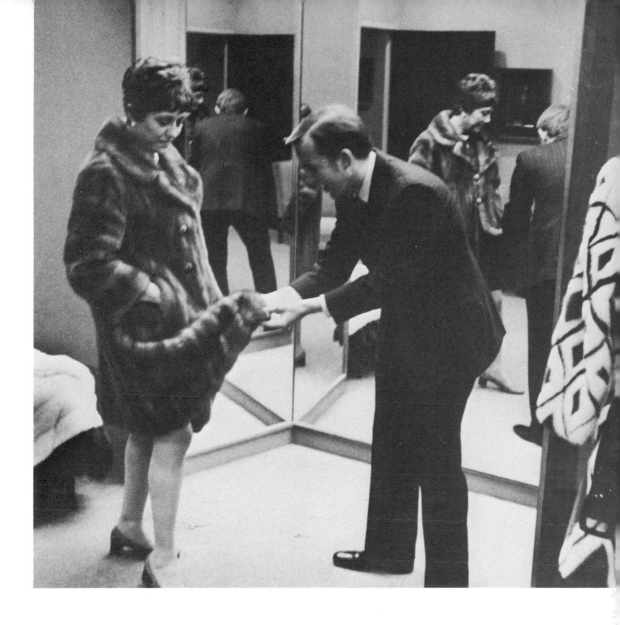

A woman buying something expensive, such as a fur, wants to feel the person selling it to her is an authority.

A customer buying wines needs a specialist's help to understand not only the foreign names but the differences among wines.

A man selling in the Pet Department should be able to explain how the animals or fish or birds or reptiles are to be fed and taken care of once the customers get them home.

If the salesperson is selling shoes, he or she should know how to make sure the customer gets the right size and fit, because this is not only a matter of comfort but of health as well.

Some customers are more difficult to deal with than others.

A major reason why Americans are the best-dressed people in the world is the mass production of our clothing. It means we can have the latest fashions for far less than they would cost if each outfit were made individually for each customer. But special fitters must frequently take measurements and mark the clothes to make them fit the individual customers.

After the fitting, these clothes are taken to the store's Alteration Department, where seamstresses and tailors make the changes indicated by the fitters.

For alterations in furs, there are separate Fur Workrooms, where specialists called "furriers" work on cutting and sewing skins.

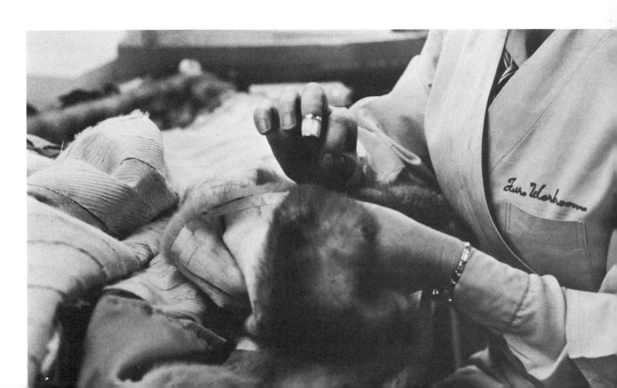

All the things a store offers for sale must be selected for it from hundreds of various manufacturers. This is done by the store's buyers who often go all over the world.

In February in Nuremberg, Germany, at the Toy Fair, a buyer selects and orders toys that will arrive in his store in time for the following Christmas season.

In Paris at the showings of the French *couturiers*, buyers from American stores select models—sometimes selling the originals in their stores, but more often turning them over to American manufacturers to mass produce in less expensive copies.

Buyers also go to other markets—to California for sportswear, to Chicago for furniture, and to New York for many things, scarves and skiis, jewelry and pajamas, handbags and hats, and hi-fis.

Then weeks or months later, from all over the world, Italy and St. Louis and India, the merchandise arrives by air and sea and train and truck to the store's Receiving and Marking Department.

People must unpack and inspect and count it to be sure that the quantities and styles and colors and sizes the manufacturer sent are in fact what the buyer ordered. This merchandise must then be steamed and pressed or polished or dusted by people who specialize in this work, and then tickets showing size and price and department and date received are printed and put on.

In only a very few stores is merchandise tested scientifically in a laboratory to see that a ball has enough bounce or a plate sufficient resistance to breakage.

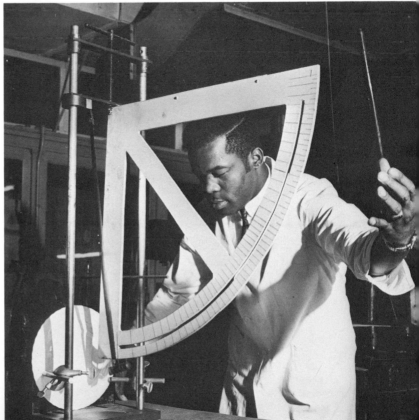

The merchandise is then sent to its proper department in the main store and the various branches. In the morning before the store opens, the salespeople are shown the new merchandise, often by the assistant buyer, who explains what is new and desirable about it.

There are in every large store, hundreds of people behind the scenes with many different duties and talents who are rarely seen or thought of by the customers. The job of some of these people is sales promotion in its various forms—creating a desire in the customer to buy something the store has to sell.

There are the artists who sketch the merchandise for the ads and the models who pose for the artists.

Then there are photographers who take the pictures sometimes used in the ads instead of sketches, and the laboratory assistants who develop and print the films.

There are copywriters who write the words in the newspaper advertisements intended to tempt the customer. Sometimes it is dreadfully difficult to think of something new to say about another outfit.

There are display artists in the store's Sales Promotion Department who create its windows and interior displays. They

have storerooms of mannequins and props and paints to help them in their work—which is really a kind of theater design. By hiding a small electric fan in the corner of a window, pulling back the hem of a raincoat with virtually invisible monofilament fishing line, and devising imaginative lighting, they can create the illusion of a storm. With paintbrush, staple gun, and hat pin, these people every week must put a new show on in the windows, to pull the pedestrians into the store. And inside the store they must create other displays to keep the customer wandering and tempted, rather than allowing him to leave the store after making his purchase.

There are style-show and fashion coordinators and models who put on shows of clothes and accessories, both in the store (on the fashion floors or in the store's dining room) and away from the store. This involves fitting the clothes on the models, children and adults, and later making sure that all the things get back to the selling departments.

A model's life is harder and less glamorous than it seems. One problem is that she acquires the taste for wearing the newest and most expensive fashions, while earning a less than extravagant salary.

A store also has a Publicity and Promotion Department which brings to the store circus clowns or ballerinas or writers or television and movie stars, whom the customers will hopefully flock in to meet and ask for autographs.

Some stores, too, have big annual events, for example a Thanksgiving Day parade, for which planning goes on all year long. Such events, of course, add to the prices a store must charge for its merchandise.

There are many other kinds of people who work behind the scenes. Clerical people keep track of what is selling. Others order the merchandise and still others see that the store's bills to its various suppliers are paid.

There are also people who try to see to it that the store is never out of basic, nonperishable items, Boy Scout badges or white sheets or black cotton thread.

Once or twice a year almost everyone in the store works overtime on weekends to count and list everything in the whole store. This is called "taking inventory." In the Major Appliance Department it is not difficult, but in the Cosmetic Department, for example, where there are thousands and thousands of small items, it is tiresome.

Most people today buy what they want, not for cash but on credit, that is, they buy something today but only pay for it over the next few months or years. A store, therefore, has many people in its Credit Department who try to determine how much credit a customer should be given; who figure the interest and service charges on these credit accounts; who send the bills out to customers every month and question the customer whose payments are late.

A store, being made up of people, makes many mistakes and must have a Complaint Department where customers can get errors corrected. The store employees who work here need steady nerves, patience, and a more than usual desire to help and understand people.

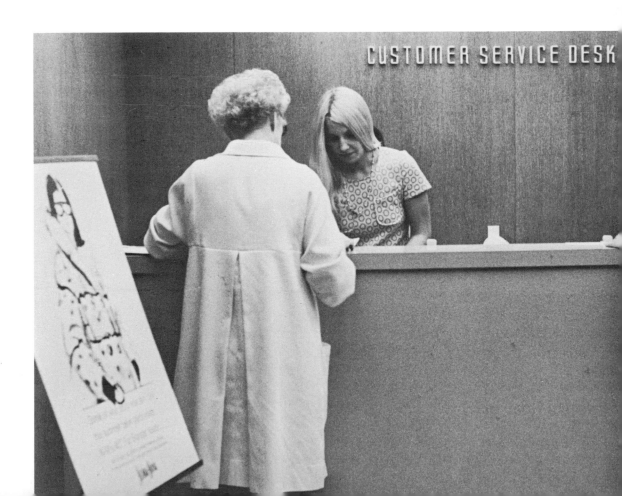

Switchboard operators, too, need a good deal of patience—but perhaps less than is needed by customers who telephone their orders into a store and must wait because the switchboards are jammed.

In the Telephone and Mail Order Department are those people who try to fill the orders of customers who prefer not to or cannot come into the store and shop in person. They must often read illegible handwriting and sometimes listen as a telephone customer angrily insists that the store advertised something when, in fact, it was advertised by another store.

Many people later send back what they have bought. There are people, therefore, who see that these returns are put back in the right department; that if the price tags have been removed, new and correct ones are put on, and that the customer receives credit for what he has returned.

Stores must guard against shoplifters and other thieves who steal merchandise, both when the store is open and at night when it is closed. During store hours there are not only uniformed guards, but also plainclothes detectives of both sexes, who mingle with the customers.

Some stores also have closed circuit television systems, over which they can watch and even photograph customers who do not know they are being watched. Thievery has been increasing for years and has now reached such a level that it makes everything sold in a store cost more than it would otherwise.

In addition to watchmen who patrol at night, some stores also use dogs because they can cover more territory than a man can and much faster. Their great sense of smell can also discover thieves hidden from view.

In addition to men and dogs, some stores have special hidden alarms and secret traps in departments where there is particularly valuable merchandise such as furs, jewelry, or coins and stamps.

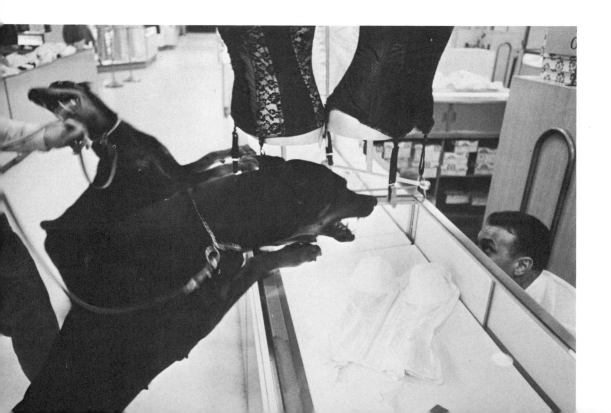

Every day a store takes in thousands of dollars in coins and bills and checks, and these must be carefully collected and counted and taken to the bank without being lost or stolen. The time when they are picked up by an armed guard and taken to the bank in an armored truck is usually varied and kept secret in order to avoid holdups.

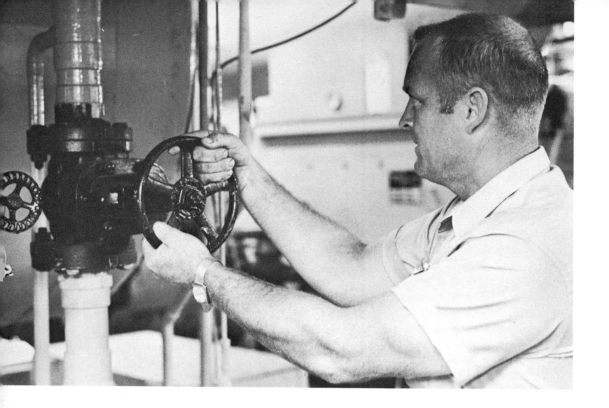

A store must have engineers and maintenance men who keep it cool in summer, warm in winter; who see that there is plenty of steam for pressing, and that fire-extinguishing and sprinkler systems, elevators, escalators, and the hundreds of machines and motors stay in good working order.

A store may have its own delivery system and delivery men, or may use a communal delivery service. It may also have its own people install and repair the stoves, washers, dryers, freezers, and television sets it sells, or may hire outside people to do these things.

There are in many stores even more specialists.

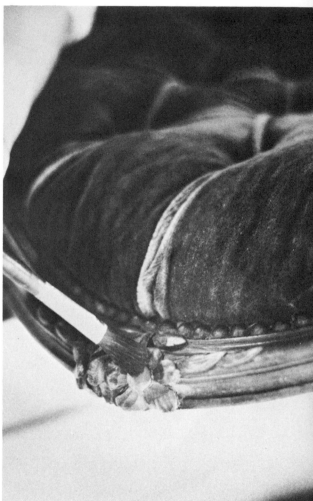

If the store has an epicurean dining room, there are cooks and chefs, and if there is a Pastry Shop, the store must have a baker.

Depending on what departments a store has, it may also employ a cabinetmaker to repair antique furniture;

an expert in retouching and restoring,

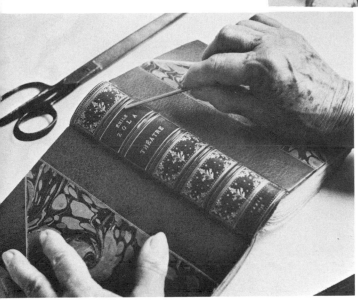

or a bookbinder, if it has a department selling rare old books and autographs.

There are printers in the store's own print shop, who make the hundreds of signs needed to tell the customer clearly, briefly, temptingly, and accurately a wide variety of facts— color, size, price, kind, where, when, how, why.

A store must keep a good crew of carpenters and electricians, not only for constant repairs, but also for almost equally constant changes. At Christmas the Toy Department must expand to many times its size during the other seasons of the year and the same is true of swim and beach wear in spring and summer.

And there are teamsters to move the fixtures and displays from the warehouses to the main store or its branches and then back to the warehouses.

There are people in every store whose job it is just to look after supplies—the tons of bags and boxes and the miles of tape and string a store needs. A few stores are especially proud of their gift and seasonal holiday wrappings and have become well known for the beauty and originality of these.

Housekeeping is an enormous job in any store for the people who collect and bale and carry off the mountains of waste that collect daily.

American stores increasingly in recent years have been selling services as well as merchandise—watch and jewelry repair, furniture reupholstering, photographic developing and printing, rug cleaning, and even automotive centers, and these departments are usually leased to specialists in such work.

Many other departments including beauty salons, barber shops, millinery departments, and travel agencies, which appear to be run by the store itself, are often in fact leased to specialists. When a store has an Interior Decorating Department or one that sells paintings and sculpture, these, too, require people with special talents and training.

There are also in every store, people whose specialty is people—hiring and firing them, training and retraining them, listening to their complaints, and choosing some for advancement. These people work in the Personnel and Training Departments.

There are also in every store the executives who make the storewide policy decisions, such as whether to handle less or more expensive merchandise; which of the many different advertising media to use and in what quantity; where and in what size and architectural style to build branch stores.

But these executives are not themselves usually the owners of the stores. Most stores are, in fact, no longer owned locally in the cities where they do business, but rather are only parts of large chains, which are owned by thousands of stockholders. The top executives are often people who worked their way up in one or more department stores.

Hopefully, these executives and all department store people bear in mind not only the needs of the employees and stockholders, but also the broader needs of the whole country in such matters as honesty of advertising and labeling, conservation of threatened species, fair and clear credit practices, and equal employment opportunities. If integrity was important in the early days of great stores, it is not less so today. It is the responsibility of the customers (certainly not the least important of the people who make a department store) to insist on such integrity.

Since the days of the Phoenician traders through the Venetians and America's early New England traders, merchants have increased people's knowledge of other people all around the world and been a part of filling human wants and needs and vanities. The people who make department stores today are a part of that tradition.